Original title:
Ode to a Peace Lily

Copyright © 2025 Creative Arts Management OÜ
All rights reserved.

Author: Matthew Whitaker
ISBN HARDBACK: 978-1-80581-877-9
ISBN PAPERBACK: 978-1-80581-404-7
ISBN EBOOK: 978-1-80581-877-9

A Floral Embrace of Stillness

In the corner, you stand so still,
With leaves that bend to every thrill.
Your white blooms, like little hats,
Make me think of fancy chats.

Dust bunnies hide, they're in despair,
For you're the star of this living layer.
With your grace, they can't compete,
You float like air, so light, so sweet.

Dancing Shadows of Grace

In the sunlight, you sway and wink,
Casting shadows that make me think.
Are you dancing or just teasing?
With every rustle, oh, so pleasing!

The cat stares down with a jealous gaze,
Wishing he had those leafy ways.
He plots and plans a daring leap,
Yet you remain, serene and deep.

The Language of Softness

Whispers of green in the room do creep,
   While I sip tea and take a leap.
   Your petals speak of tender care,
   While I pretend you're a rare heir.

Elegance in Every Curve

With curves that make the best of art,
You offer calmness, play your part.
And while I giggle at your stance,
You remind me life can be a dance!

Nature's Soft Song

In corner's grasp, a leafy mate,
With petals pure, it doesn't hate.
A houseplant's dream, a carefree sigh,
It opens wide, but never flies.

Its secret weapon? Dust-free care,
Just like my socks, it loves the air.
Whispers soft, in green attire,
Forget the broom, meet this empire!

Veils of Pure Tranquility

With each new leaf, it struts its stuff,
A diva plant, but never tough.
Swaying gently, it plays the part,
Of nature's calm, and not too smart.

It drinks in light, its favorite drink,
While I fumble, caught in the brink.
Hands off my snacks, dear leafy friend,
Let's not pretend we can't just blend!

The Peaceful Bloom's Promise

Oh gentle bloom, a peace parade,
Your elegance is not delayed.
I whisper tales, you nod and wink,
Oh, what a bond! You make me think.

Green thumb legends whisper near,
You thrive on jokes and even beer.
Promise me a laugh each day,
In our green world, let's play!

Petals in the Moonlight

Beneath the moon, it sways so bright,
A leafy ghost in silver light.
Poking fun at my bad jokes,
Who knew plants can tease like folks?

Filter the sun, sip water neat,
Roots have rhythm, moving to beat.
Let's dance tonight, you and I,
With blooms that reach for the night sky.

Dreams Cradled by Foliage

In the corner, a plant stands still,
Dreaming big, with such quiet will.
Leaves like umbrellas, shading my thought,
Whispers of wisdom, or just a spot?

What secrets you hold, dear leafy friend,
Do you giggle at the mess I blend?
A bit of dust, a splash of my tea,
I swear you're plotting a plan for me!

Silent Guardians of the Home

A sentinel green, perched high and proud,
Watching my antics, a judgmental crowd.
Through spills and thrills, steadfast you stare,
Companion to chaos, without a care.

You drink from my troubles, roots deep in the ground,
With every mishap, you still stand around.
If plants could laugh, you'd chortle in glee,
As I trip over slippers, who falls next? Me!

The Radiance of Gentle Spirit

Petals like smiles, spreading some cheer,
You lighten my heart when my worries near.
A don't-need-a-makeup kind of grace,
Even in chaos, you find your place.

At dinner you watch, with a subtle wink,
You seem to know when I'm on the brink.
With every misstep, I hear your silent shout,
"Just keep it together, don't freak out!"

A Sanctuary of White

In the living room, a soft, white glow,
You brighten the day, when it's all moving slow.
Stuck at my desk, you provide some flair,
A comical contrast to my vacant stare.

Perhaps you're the muse of my desk-bound plight,
Spilling puns like petals, a hilarious sight.
With every new bloom, you invite a grin,
In this jungle of papers, let the fun begin!

Mornings Wrapped in Green

Awake to green with sleepy eyes,
The little plant yawns and sighs,
It's time to sip from morning dew,
While pondering all that it can do.

Its leaves dance in the morning light,
Winking at the cat in fright,
Who thinks that plants plot in the night,
But they just dream of snacks—what a sight!

Sighs of a Peaceful Heart

In corners where the light is soft,
The peace lily sways and drifts aloft,
It hums a tune, so sweetly bright,
While plotting world peace, what a sight!

Neighbors hear the noise, they smile,
As plants debate the luckiest style,
Of how to grow and stretch and gleam,
In this sunny room, a botanical dream.

The Elegy of Gentle Hues

Oh, gentle hues in leafy folds,
Whispering secrets of lives untold,
They gossip quietly about the sun,
And how to best have endless fun.

With petals sharp and leaves so broad,
They cheer for each other, a leafy squad,
In the battle of best indoor decor,
Each green champion dreams of wanting more!

Blooms Beckoning Stillness

The blooms beckon with a curious plea,
'Join us in tranquility!' they agree,
While squirrels outside throw seeds like confetti,
The peace lily just giggles, ever so petty.

So if you seek a laugh or cheer,
Just whisper to plants, they will always hear,
In their lush world of vibrant spree,
They'll crack a joke, just wait, you'll see!

Embrace of the Indoor Sanctuary

In the corner, you sway with grace,
An overachiever in our small space.
You sip the sunlight, take a bow,
Softest diva—what a show-off now!

Dust bunnies stare, quite mortified,
You steal the spotlight, they try to hide.
In the battle of green, you take the chance,
A leafy dance, oh what a prance!

Visitors gawk, you know it's true,
While they admire, I roll my eyes at you.
With your bright petals, smug and spry,
I'm worried you'll think you can fly!

Still, I adore this houseplant friend,
With your quirks, the giggles never end.
So here's to you, my leafy delight,
May your antics make our days so bright!

Unveiling Nature's Whisper

Oh, dear plant, with a wink and a smile,
You're the star of my indoor style.
Your mystique's a puzzle, I swear it's true,
Washed and polished, who does that for you?

You soak in the water, like it's a bath,
Do you practice your poses, or share a laugh?
Each new leaf, a secret revealed,
Like a plant-based movie, you've sneakily healed.

Your style's so chic, it makes me feel dull,
With each leafy layer, I find myself full.
Yet when you throw shade, it's not the fun kind,
Shutting my plants out—oh, what a bind!

So here's to your charm and delightful flair,
In this wild jungle of indoor air.
Keep whispering secrets, keep shining bright,
Our goofy duet, a marvelous sight!

In the Presence of Peace

Peaceful one, with your green fingertips,
You waltz through my home, making tips and trips.
You chase away worries, with hardly a frown,
Yet potting you? Oh, I'll need a crown!

Your simplicity shines, but oh, what a plight,
You've made my other plants look less bright.
While I grow old, in plant dad disgrace,
You just smile, a constant soft face.

Let's keep it real, you diva of ease,
With your slow-paced vibe, you're a tease.
Your friends are jealous of your cheap upkeep,
While I am here—barely awake from sleep!

But with every glance at your peace-loving leaf,
I find solace and, sometimes, great relief.
So prance on, dear plant, keep the chaos afar,
You're the tranquil peace near my wild home bazaar!

Lullaby of the Leaf

Sing, little leaf, your lullaby song,
With tiny vibrations, you can't go wrong.
You dance in the breeze, all soft and snug,
A comedic star, my potted bug!

When I tell you my worries, you nod your green head,
In unspoken comfort, you spout what I dread.
With a flick of your fronds, and a glimmer of light,
You turn my troubles into a delight!

But beware of the cat, oh what a clutz,
Leaping and bounding, a real furry butt!
One swift swipe, you could end up on floors,
And your peace-loving giggle becomes loud roars.

Nevertheless, dear plant, I'll hold you near,
Through laughter and chaos, we'll persevere.
So here's to our folly, and your leafy reprieve,
A whimsical tale in the lull of the eve!

Reflections of Inner Harmony

In the corner sits you, with grace and flair,
A leafy chap, bringing cheer everywhere.
You sway in the breeze, a dance so wily,
Even my cat thinks you're a bit silly.

Raise a brow, oh green pet, don't be blind,
To the laughter you bring to a home well-defined.
With a flick of your leaves, you spread joy and fun,
Who knew a plant could be such a pun?

Nature's Whispered Caress

Oh you, with your blossoms, so pure and white,
At night when I'm restless, you shine so bright.
Your petals are soft, your humor too grand,
Dream on, dear flower, you're part of the band.

With a giggle and nod, you keep up the game,
A joke in the stillness, you do stake your claim.
Should I accidentally trip on a shoe,
You laugh it off with your leaf of bright hue!

The Lullaby of Leaves

Slumbering softly in your leafy retreat,
You hum a sweet tune that's ever so neat.
While I pack my worries in tight little bags,
You wiggle and giggle, oh, how my heart sags.

Make room for the laughter, my dear little friend,
For joy's just a tickle, let the fun never end.
You whisper to dreamers, come join in the cheer,
What's life without humor? It's awfully drear!

Still Waters

You stand quite regal, like an emerald queen,
Creating a calm in the chaos unseen.
With a glance so tranquil, you brush off the stress,
While I daily question your lack of a dress.

But who needs the glam when you've got all the charm?
A touch of your elegance keeps my life warm.
In the stillness, my friend, I take in the scene,
With a chuckle, a sigh, you're my leafy caffeine.

Gentle Blooms

Among the clutter, you bloom with such grace,
A soft giggle echoes, filling this space.
Catching lost moments like butterflies do,
While I swear you must have a joke or two.

You sprout little smiles with every new leaf,
Laughter and blooms are my daily relief.
Oh peace-loving plant, you hush all the fuss,
In a world full of chaos, you're simply a plus!

Tranquil Embrace

In the corner sits a green delight,
With petals white, it steals the light.
Dust collects where sunshine beams,
A silent guardian of my dreams.

I spill my coffee, it gives a sigh,
"Worry not, my friend, just let it dry."
With every spill, a gentle grin,
It hugs the mess, invites me in.

Leaves perk up at my morning tune,
"Can we dance?" it seems to croon.
With every sway, it holds its ground,
In my chaos, calm is found.

So here we are, just two of us,
In this room, we make a fuss.
With laughter shared and worries quelled,
In this embrace, our secrets held.

Nature's Calm Companion

A leafy friend with a quiet charm,
Bringing peace, with no alarm.
When I trip and nearly fall,
It just giggles, standing tall.

Morning light makes it shine bright,
"Look at me!" it seems to write.
As I stumble through my days,
It whispers jokes in leafy ways.

When I'm loud, it takes a bow,
"More volume? Okay, I'll allow!"
For every joke and every jest,
My calm companion knows me best.

As I pass by with my fuss,
It chuckles softly, "What's the rush?"
In this dance of friendship true,
Nature smiles and I giggle too.

The Luminous Calm

In my room, a glow resides,
With white blooms that loves to hide.
From the chaos, it takes a stand,
A peaceful presence, gentle hand.

When I speak in silly tones,
It nods along, no need for phones.
"Tell me more of your grand plans,"
It seems to say, sans demands.

Every time I bring the snacks,
Its leaves reach out, no silly acts.
"May I have a crumb?" it pleads,
In this home, it's filled with needs.

As night falls, it shuts its eyes,
Dreaming dreams under starry skies.
With giggles shared, we end the day,
My luminous calm, forever stay.

Whispers of Tranquil Green

A plant so calm, it takes its stand,
Sipping rain and feeling grand.
In a corner, it lounges with a sigh,
Quiet watch over the world passing by.

Its leaves, a hat for the sunlight's tease,
Laughing at worries like a gentle breeze.
When dust gets close, it waves 'hello',
Then shouts, "I'm your best friend, don't you know?"

Each petal a secret, each nod a boost,
Hearing my tales, it's an excellent roost.
"Why worry too much?" it seems to play,
"I've got your back in a leafy way!"

So here's to the plant with a smile so wide,
In the silly dance of life, it takes pride.
With whispers of joy, it grows and it leans,
A quirky friend clad in tranquil greens.

Serenity in Petals

With a wink and a tilt, it struts like a king,
Swaying softly, as if to sing.
"Today is a good day to chill," it says,
While I munch my snacks and gaze in a daze.

It knows my secrets, but never tells,
Behind those petals, it quietly dwells.
"Did you just say 'water'?" it grins with glee,
"I'm thriving here, buddy, just look at me!"

Sometimes I think it's plotting a plan,
To take over the couch with its leafy fan.
But who wouldn't want a grand ol' time,
With a plant that sways like it's doing a rhyme?

So here's to serenity wrapped in green dress,
This plant's my partner in harmless jest.
A laugh in the silence of afternoon's glow,
Among the petals, all worries let go.

The Calm Within the Leaf

In the living room, it's a superstar,
A peace-keeper, with no hint of bizarre.
"Hey there!" it whispers, as I walk by,
Dropping worries, like a tight-lipped spy.

Its leaves do yoga, stretching with grace,
Seeking sunlight, it finds its place.
"Too stressed?" it chuckles, "Let's take a break,
I'll listen to you, for old friendship's sake."

Each frond's a poem, written in green,
Tales of tranquility, calm, and serene.
As I chat away, it nods in delight,
Laughing so softly, shining so bright.

So let's raise a toast to this plant, my friend,
In the garden of life, it's the sweet blend.
With calm in the leaves and a wink in the air,
Together we dance, without a care.

Blooming Beneath Quietness

There's magic here, in the hush of the morn,
With petals that smile, not a hint of scorn.
"Why rush?" it implores in a delicate way,
"Just bloom where you're planted, let's seize the day!"

With a wave to the dust, it plays in light,
Balancing joy and the sofa's slight bite.
"I make air fresh, while you munch your snack,
No need for a hurry, I've got your back!"

Whispers of whimsy swirl through the air,
In a dance of silence, it's without a care.
"Next time you trip, blame it on me,
I'm the plant that giggles, can't you see?"

So here's to my peace flower, clever and spry,
In the rhythm of life, it'll always comply.
With laughter and calm, it's a bloom divine,
In this quiet chaos, it's perfectly fine.

Guardian of Tranquility

In the corner it stands, quite bold,
Green leaves whisper tales untold.
A sentinel for my chaotic plight,
With roots so deep, it holds on tight.

A gentle face, in white it beams,
Muffled laughter in my dreams.
It mocks my worries, gives them a shove,
Like a friend who knows the strength of love.

Oh, how it sways, with rhythm so fine,
Dancing with dust as if it were wine.
A plant with sass, a quirky grace,
In its embrace, I find my place.

So raise a toast to the leafy knight,
Who cheers me on with all its might.
The guardian of my tranquil zone,
In its company, I'm never alone.

The Calm After the Storm

When chaos rages, I start to sweat,
But then I spy my favorite pet.
With petals white, it starts to glow,
A reminder that calm will surely flow.

It chuckles softly, in the breeze,
While I'm tangled up in a life of fees.
"Breathe easy now," it seems to say,
"Trouble's just a game; let's laugh and play."

After the thunder, here comes the light,
This little diva, oh, what a sight!
Hiding the mess of my wild, loud day,
With each petal, it sweeps woes away.

So here's to peace, in all its charms,
Wrapped in leaves, in nature's arms.
After the storm, it winks at me wide,
For in its stillness, I'll always abide.

Petals of Stillness

In the morning light, it greets the day,
With petals that giggle, come what may.
"Who needs a spa?" it seems to declare,
"When you've got me, your fresh air bear!"

The world spins wild, like a disco ball,
Yet here it stands, not bothered at all.
I'm busy stressing, but it just smiles,
Teaching serenity, with minimal trials.

It's the one plant that truly can thrive,
In my little chaos, it's very alive.
I swear it's plotting to publish a book,
On how to chill, with just one look.

So here's to its wisdom, wrapped in green,
The irony of peace—so pure and clean.
In every leaf, a joke to unfurl,
With petals of stillness, it conquers the world!

Where Light Meets Leaf

Sunlight spills on emerald skin,
As if it knows where to begin.
Each glimmer brightens the somber game,
"Come sit with me!" it laughs, without shame.

In playful shadows, it stretches wide,
A light chaser with leafy pride.
"Life's just a dance," I hear it say,
"Join my leafy ballet, come what may!"

With such a presence, it takes the floor,
While I'm just here, fumbling for more.
It teases the gloom with a radiant twist,
A green companion I simply can't resist.

So toast to the sunshine, to moments brief,
Where light meets leaf, and offers relief.
For in this dance, we twirl and spin,
A botanical jest, where peace begins!

Tranquil Resonance in Every Petal.

In the corner, you stand so bright,
A leafy friend in morning light.
You soak up water with such glee,
Pretending you're a sipping tea!

With blooms so white, like clouds of fluff,
You nod your head; we get enough.
But watch out now, don't spill the beans,
Your secret's out: you're planning scenes!

You stretch and sway, a leafy dance,
Making each room a leafy romance.
But step too close and you'll just know,
Your leaves will flick, a leafy show!

Oh, peace you share so generously,
Though cat wants to take a bite, you see.
But you stand tall with silent grace,
Cue the laughter, the party's base!

Whispers in the Green

Whispering secrets, oh so light,
You make my worries take to flight.
A chat with you is always sweet,
Even if you just sip on feet.

You're a listener that never yawns,
Not a peep as the hour dawns.
But call too loud, and you just might,
Throw shade at me with all your might!

You drink the sun, you sip the rain,
To think of you gives me a pain.
Proudly standing, never a frown,
Making Mondays wear a crown!

So here's a cheer to leafy friends,
Where giggles start and laughter bends.
In every room, you steal the show,
With quiet charm and sneaky glow!

Serenity's Silent Bloom

In your presence, woes take a bow,
With a twist of leaf, oh wow!
You bloom and boast, so pure and neat,
Just don't forget your playful feet!

You sway like dancers on a stage,
A green delight that calms the rage.
But let's be honest, please don't pout,
When cat decides to find you out!

The way you whisper with your leaves,
Makes me chuckle; I can't believe!
You nod and wink, so sly and bold,
In your company, I can't be cold!

Yet here you stand, so sweet and pure,
A plant of peace, that's for sure.
With every bloom, you brightened my day,
Even when cat thinks it's a buffet!

Elegance of the Pure White

Oh, elegant friend, pure as snow,
Your beauty puts on quite a show.
In every leaf, there's joy galore,
And a sprinkle of mischief we adore!

Your petals wave like silly flags,
While outside world just sags and drags.
You boast of peace, but wait, oh no,
When cat decides it's time to go!

You lift my spirit with simple grace,
An indoor star in this cozy space.
But here's a truth, let's give a wink,
You've got a heart that doesn't sink!

So here's to you, my leafy queen,
In every giggle and every scene.
You remind me of joy without the fuss,
In this home of laughter, it's just us!

Reveries in Botanical Silence

In the corner, she stands so proud,
With leaves that sway, never too loud.
Whispering secrets of sunlight's dance,
She nods along, in a leafy trance.

Her blooms, like mimes, in quiet white,
Plotting antics, what a sight!
When dust bunnies leap and cats go wild,
She just giggles, nature's child.

Beneath her gaze, the sunbeams play,
Cards and grass clippings on display.
Oh, how she chuckles at our fuss,
While sipping water, just to adjust.

Her tranquil charm, a jest divine,
As we talk to her - she sips her wine.
In silence, she stirs chaos and jest,
The peace lily wins, we're all just guests.

The Harmonious Petal

In a pot of secrets, she lingers near,
With petals so calm, you'd think she'd cheer.
She watches us bumble with chores to do,
As we trip over shoes, a classic view.

Her ghostly white blooms mock our stress,
Swaying gentle, like a peaceful mess.
As we scramble for socks, on a wild chase,
She smiles politely, oh what a grace!

Every sneeze from the dusty shelf,
She rolls her eyes, calls it bad health.
While we're ranting about life's little quirks,
She keeps her chill, amidst our works.

Finally, we pause, and take in her glee,
In her botanical wisdom, we find the key.
No need to fret, while she blooms on free,
For a petal with humor holds the best spree.

A Serene Palette of White

In the sun's embrace, she softly beams,
With a halo of green, in laughter it seems.
Her petals wave like flags at a feast,\nInviting us closer, to chat with the beast.

A mishap occurs with the watering can,
Oh dear, there she goes, a soggy plan!
Craving our laughter, she perks up her face,
Bringing serenity into the wild race.

Around her, the world spins in a blur,
But she holds her ground; she will not stir.
Beneath her watch, we fumble and play,
In this laughter-filled chaos, she's here to stay.

So let's raise our voices, craft a cheer,
To the lily that stands, our funny dear.
For in her calmness, mayhem ignites,
She dances with joy, in soft moonlight rites.

The Art of Listening to Nature

In the garden of whispers, a bloom of delight,
Where peace lily flirts with the morning light.
She's a botanist's dream, with a witty twist,
Eavesdropping on ants, who couldn't resist.

While we grumble about the next big task,
She chuckles softly, "Just take off that mask!"
For in her soft shade, nothing's amiss,
Every sigh and each laugh, a botanical kiss.

Her leaves catch our words like a warm summer breeze,
Bringing laughter to daisies and calming the trees.
With a petite little smirk, she sways with flair,
While we argue about who forgot to share.

So here's to the peace that she brings with style,
In her harmony, we find our own smile.
A lily on the shelf, with mischief bright,
Teaching us joy in the softest light.

The Solace of Indoor Blooms

In the corner sits a leafy friend,
A peaceful plant that won't offend.
It whispers 'chill' with every glance,
And waters my life with a funny dance.

With petals bright, it sways with glee,
A funny sight, just look and see!
I trip on roots, and it just smiles,
Sipping on love, it hosts wild styles.

Tending to it brings giggles loud,
This serene queen, it makes me proud.
It wipes my brow when I lose my key,
Oh, peace is here, how can this be?

Most times it's calm; sometimes it sighs,
Its humor glimmers in gentle highs.
A silent laugh, a whispering cheer,
This leafy friend, forever near.

Peace Unfurled in Petals

Oh flower fair with vibrant flair,
You catch the light just like a stare.
When friends drop by and chatter flows,
You soak it all; nobody knows.

With blossoms bold, you spear the air,
A stand-up act without a care.
I joke and prance around your shade,
You sip your tea; no plans are made.

Leafy green, your humor's sly,
In creased folds, you gently lie.
Cracking jokes in silence, true,
A jesting peace we always knew.

In moments shared, you steal my heart,
With every leaf, you play your part.
Oh, how you bloom in laughter bright,
A chuckle tucked in pure delight.

Floral Emissaries of Calm

Oh, gentle stalk with blooms so white,
You keep my stress levels light.
A true diplomat of flowery cheer,
In moments of chaos, you appear.

Your leaves wave hi as I walk by,
A daily chat with no need to pry.
You nod and chuckle, a calming host,
In every corner, I love you most.

When slackers come, and tempers flare,
You puff your petals, 'Don't you dare!'
And in your shade, we laugh and play,
With floral flair, you save the day.

Your vibe is chill; your grin's so wide,
With you beside, there's nothing to hide.
Oh peaceful plant, you shine so bright,
In every room, you are pure light.

The Essence of Repose

In leafy twists, your humor glows,
A leafy comedy; who really knows?
You sway and tease with subtle grace,
A plant, a friend, in our shared space.

When life gets loud and colors clash,
You giggle softly, making a splash.
With every leaf, you shimmy and sway,
A floral jester in disarray.

In brief respite, you ease my mind,
With you around, I'm less confined.
Oh lumpy friend, my floral glee,
Your leafy charm has saved me free.

From every corner, joy does bloom,
In your embrace, I find my room.
A restful smile in every hour,
Unfurling peace, my leafy flower.

The Allure of a Soft Bloom

In the corner of the room, it sways,
A plant with style that always plays,
Its leaves like dancers, waltzing free,
As if they know the way to glee.

Every petal boasts a brilliant shine,
Pretending to be fancy wine,
"Drink me up", they giggle with zest,
While I just sigh and give it my best.

Around the pot, dust bunnies scurry,
But this green beauty is never in a hurry,
With blooms that look like soft clouds above,
It rolls its eyes at the lack of love.

Yet somehow, in silence, it brightens my day,
With whispers of joy in a leafy ballet,
So here's to the plant with the greatest flair,
The charming bloom that doesn't seem to care.

Elysium in the Heart of Green

Nestled among the elbowing leaves,
A soft saint radiates vibes, it believes,
With a smug smile, it takes a stand,
Charming plants, like it's grandest band.

The cat thinks it's a throne of grace,
While I'm convinced it takes up space,
Yet its quirks make me cheerfully drool,
A diva with roots that bends every rule.

It teases the sun and strokes the breeze,
Convinced they're just waiting to please,
As I water it daily, it makes a fuss,
While I'm just hoping it won't start to rust.

In a jungle of clutter, it rises high,
A comedic gem, that's not shy,
In the heart of green, it claims its throne,
A diva of nature, forever alone.

A Breath of Whispering Petals

In the still of the morning light,
Whispering petals flaunt their might,
"Look at me!" they seem to shout,
While the other plants just pout.

Caffeine cups huddle in their haze,
But this bloom brightens dullest days,
It stretches out to giggle at me,
Mocking my efforts to drink my tea.

The jokes it tells in budding blooms,
About my hair and morning glooms,
Why must you laugh when you're so sweet?
Oh, soft petals, can't take this heat!

Yet each time I walk past your grin,
You lift my spirits without a din,
In your company, I silently snicker,
For in your charm, my heart grows quicker.

The Dance of Peaceful Spirits

In the quiet of dusk, they begin to sway,
Those petals prance, in a quirky ballet,
While I sit laughing, feeling a fool,
As if this plant holds the world's biggest school.

They whisper secrets as night begins,
Playful jests, like cheeky kin,
"Your socks don't match, did you forget?"
The spirit of humor in leafy etiquette.

As I try to ignore their cheeky snark,
They twirl 'round the pot, like a lark,
Charging my heart with laughter's dance,
In a leafy world, I'm caught in a trance.

Alas, the blossoms, through giggles interlace,
Bring joy in this pot, my charming space,
With a wink and a nod, they claim their estate,
In a creamy white costume, oh, isn't it great?

The Unsung Protector

In the corner, it stands so coy,
Guarding secrets, like a stealthy toy.
With leaves so green, it casts a spell,
A silent guardian, a leafy sentinel.

Who knew a plant could hold such sway?
It whispers, 'Keep worries at bay!'
With every dust speck that lands on its hue,
It giggles, 'I'll clean that; I'm here for you!'

The cat walks by, gives a curious stare,
As blooms stretch up like they haven't a care.
In this household, my peace lily reigns,
A comical ruler with no earthly chains.

Serenity in the Shadows

In dim-lit corners, chic and sleek,
My peace lily hovers, not one to speak.
Its presence is calm, yet there's so much fun,
You'd almost think it's plotting a pun.

It flickers with laughter as new leaves unfurl,
Pretending to dance in a leafy swirl.
With soil as its throne, it rules this quaint nook,
Shushes the chaos, with just one look.

Each droop of a leaf brings a chuckle or two,
As if saying, 'Hey buddy, I can chill too!'
So here's to the plant, with humor so sly,
A shadow of laughter, oh my oh my!

A Dance of Calmness

Amid the clutter, it takes to the stage,
Opening petals, it's pure plant rage!
It twirls and it sways, with so much grace,
A leafy performance in this tiny space.

I swear it can laugh, with a wink of its leaf,
Turning my chaos into comic relief.
As I hurriedly dash, all huff and all puff,
It chuckles softly, 'You're trying too tough!'

In the spotlight of sunlight, it shines all day,
With a presence so grand, it knows how to play.
A dance of calmness, who knew it was true?
Just look at my peace lily, it's here for you!

Nurturing Stillness

There's a stillness that giggles in every bloom,
A green little jester dispelling all gloom.
It takes care of me, though it's just a plant,
With petals that sway, like my favorite chant.

Dust gathers round, but does it complain?
No way! It just laughs, 'I'm a soil-champion's gain!'
While I fumble and fuss, it just stands there with flair,
Quietly nurturing without any care.

A nurturer strange, with roots in the ground,
This plant knows how to joke, never a frown.
So here's to the lily, in all of its glory,
A funny little co-star in my leafy story.

Blossoms of Inner Peace

In the corner, she stands quite still,
With leaves so green, oh what a thrill!
Her blooms like clouds, they sway and dance,
In this house, she's found her chance.

She drinks up water, just a sip,
While I forget to give her a trip,
Yet still she smiles, her petals bright,
A symbol of calm in morning light.

Neighbors peek in with curious eyes,
Wondering how she never cries,
Amidst my chaos, clutter, and noise,
She's the queen, while I'm just a poise.

Her roots are deep, her laughter loud,
In a pot, she's secretly proud,
With every bloom, a giggle she sends,
In my space, she's the life it lends.

The Whispering Petal

In a sunny spot, she takes her throne,
A flower that never feels alone,
With a little light and love to grow,
She whispers secrets that only she knows.

Her petals wave like they just can't wait,
To share a joke or maybe a date,
With passing bugs who pause and stare,
Is it comedy or floral despair?

Each morning blooms a brand new jest,
She chuckles, saying, 'Not like the rest!'
With vines that tangle like funny hair,
Her humor grows, besides the care.

Though I tend to spill dirt here and there,
Her beauty shines, beyond compare,
In every leaf, a grin does grow,
With this diva, my heart's aglow.

Haven of Pure Delight

Here in my home, a plant prevails,
With a friendly face, she never fails,
To brighten up the dullest day,
A comedian in green, come what may!

She winks and nods, oh what a sight,
Each morning brings a petal fight!
With dust bunnies and socks that stray,
She just giggles and sways all day.

My friends all ask, 'What's her secret?
To bloom so bright while I'm in deficit?'
A pot of humor, a dash of grace,
This lily laughs right in my face.

Her presence feels like a sunny hug,
In her green peace, I'm forever snug,
With every laugh, my soul takes flight,
In her haven, everything seems right.

Guardian of the Gentle Heart

She guards my heart with leafy charm,
With a gentle sway, she means no harm,
A sentinel of smiles, what a treat,
Her calming essence can't be beat.

When life gets wild, she rolls her eyes,
And says, 'Just breathe, don't fret or cry!'
With a twinkle in her leafy gaze,
She keeps the chaos in a maze.

'You thought you'd drown?' she seems to say,
'Just look at me, I'm green all day!'
With petals soft and laughter grand,
She's the wisdom at my command.

So here's to her, my leafy sprite,
In this abode, she's pure delight,
A garden jester, all so spry,
With every bloom, she lifts me high.

Light's Dance on Petal Tips

In sunlight's glow, they sway and spin,
Whispering secrets, where do I begin?
A dance of light on silky green,
Petals twirl like a ballerina queen.

Each morning, they stretch and yawn wide,
Flirting with shadows, they're unclassified.
A giggle here, a rustle there,
In a slim vase, they don't have a care.

They peek at the cat, who gives a snore,
Seeing the sights from the window's floor.
"Is that a squirrel? Oh what a thrill!"
"Just ignore it, and enjoy the chill!"

In this quirky dance, we find pure glee,
Who knew houseplants could bring such esprit?
With petals that glisten in the radiant day,
They brighten our lives in their funny way.

The Guardian of Serenity

In silence, they stand like a bossy knight,
Guarding the room with petals so white.
"I'll protect your calm from the wildest storm,
With me around, you'll feel safe and warm."

A plant with a purpose, a leaf of might,
"Do sip your tea, and dim that bright light!"
With a flourish, they save us from stress,
"Feel free to nap; I'll handle the mess!"

Who knew a lily could part the dread?
While I fret and fume, they nod their head.
"Just take a chill, toss your worries aside,
Trust me, dear friend, I'll be your guide."

So here's to this guardian, bold and spry,
In moments of chaos, they never cry.
With a wink and a sway, they gently decree,
"Let's find some laughter, just follow me!"

A Refuge of Blooming Calm

Nestled in corners, soft as a sigh,
A refuge of calm in a world that's awry.
Each petal's a pillow, a chair for a muse,
"Rest your weary thoughts; here, you can snooze!"

Sipping coffee, I gaze at their grace,
"Join me for tea? Let's slow down the pace!"
While chaos outside rattles and rolls,
In their gentle presence, I find my goals.

As my worries drift like clouds made of foam,
This plant whispers softly, "You're always home."
They snicker at troubles, with elegance so sly,
"Let's laugh at the madness; it's good to comply!"

In this cozy retreat, where silliness reigns,
We dance through the day, forgetting our pains.
With delicate leaves, they inspire delight,
In a bloom of pure joy, everything feels right.

Tenderness in Each Leaf

With a gentle touch, they wave hello,
Each leaf wears a smile, puts on a show.
"Please don't ignore me, I'm lovely and keen!"
A soft little plant with a heart that gleans.

Petals like hugs, wrapping me tight,
In the chaos of life, they bring pure light.
"Chill out a bit, it's a wild old ride,
With me by your side, there's nothing to hide!"

Skits of leaf dances when breezes blow through,
"Can I borrow your humor? Here, try a few!"
The bending and swaying, like playful friends,
Whispering joy that never quite ends.

So here's to you, dear leafy delight,
Each hour with you feels more than just right.
With laughter and tenderness, find space to believe,
In the magic of moments, we'll endlessly weave.

The Quiet Reflection

In the corner sits a plant,
With leaves that quietly chant.
It watches me spill my tea,
And chuckles, 'You can't blame me!'

I sneak a snack, a cookie here,
It sways with laughter, my dear sphere.
'Your crumbs are mine, oh what a treat!'
I've met my match; it's tough to beat!

A confident stance, no doubt it flaunts,
While I do my wobbly dance of haunts.
Yet every eye roll it gives my way,
Is just a plant's cheeky way to play!

So here we are, a duo quite strange,
In this wild world, we laugh and change.
Oh peace lily, my leafy jest,
Together we'll conquer this household quest!

Soft Luminescence

In the morning, soft and bright,
You cuddle up to morning light.
A gentle glow, a silent roar,
"Oh no, not another boring chore!"

With pots and soil, strange smells abound,
You roll your leaves, looking around.
'Water me now, or watch me droop,'
I sigh and think, 'It's just a coop!'

Your glossy charm, it cannot hide,
You tease the sun, oh the pride!
While I fumble with your care,
You sip my coffee, unaware!

You've caught me nodding, half asleep,
With roots that seem to silently creep.
A soft nudge says, 'Let's have some fun!'
In your leafy world, there's never a pun!

Sanctuary in Bloom

Within these walls, a joke does bloom,
A leafy sage in plastic gloom.
You know my secrets, oh so dear,
"I won't tell—just give me beer!"

Each day you comfort, still and sly,
Listening to my silly sigh.
"More sunlight, please!" I plead with woe,
You just roll your eyes, "Oh, go slow!"

With every laugh and every frown,
You stand so tall, never down.
A sanctuary in twisted green,
From every disaster, you intervene!

Oh how we dance in kitchen hues,
Holding on to our playful views.
We toast to plants, to life, to scheme,
In this bloom, we dare to dream!

Breath of the House

You're the breath of this little space,
Masked in green, a leafy face.
When guests arrive, you play it cool,
"Just here to breathe, don't be a fool!"

With roots so deep, yet mischief high,
You shake your leaves and wave goodbye.
A champion of calm in my messy den,
"Don't stress, my friend; just breathe again!"

You soak up worries, inhale the cares,
While I trip on love and tangled affairs.
Through laughter and tears, we strut and sway,
"Life's a trip, now let's play!"

In our chaos, you stand so true,
A staring plant—oh what to do?
With every smile, you draw me near,
Breath of the house, my dear plant cheer!

A Hymn for the Gentle Spirit

In a pot, you sit so proud,
A leafy crown, not too loud.
Whispering jokes in shades of green,
The quietest queen we've ever seen.

You drink from rain, and bask in light,
Chasing away the dust and fright.
With every droop, we hear your laugh,
A leafy sprite on a leafy path.

When friends come by, they stop to gawk,
You're the gossip in the plant world talk.
"Look at her pose, so calm, so chill!"
Yet, we know you've got some sass to spill.

Oh gentle spirit, take a bow,
You teach us peace; we're here, somehow.
With stems like arms, you hold us tight,
In the dance of a soft, calming night.

The Flower That Knows No Strife

In a world of chaos, you stand so still,
No raging storms, no need for will.
Your blossoms smile with pure delight,
As if you've never had a fight.

You silently judge our daily woes,
While sipping water, nobody knows.
The zen master of the flora land,
With roots so deep, you make a stand.

Neighbors may bicker, but you just sigh,
"Why add drama? Just let it lie!"
You wrangle peace from every quirk,
And in your gaze, we all go berserk.

So raise a glass to your lush green cheer,
The neighbor's envy, you have no fear.
In your tranquil glow, all strife dissipates,
Oh peace-prophet plant, you steal the fates!

Harmony in Softness

Petals unfurl, a lush embrace,
In your warmth, we find our place.
"Don't be too loud," you always say,
"Just chill with me and pass the day."

With a wink, you greet the light,
In delicate tones, you're quite the sight.
Every morning, you raise a leaf,
"Calmness is key, don't dwell in grief."

As others squabble, you sway in ease,
The life of the party with perky tease.
Why shout and scream when all can flow?
You twirl with grace, putting on a show.

So here's to you, a gentle sage,
Teaching us all to act our age.
Your leafy antics, a comic delight,
Bringing us giggles with all your might.

Graceful Solitude

In quiet corners, you take your seat,
Radiating charm, oh so sweet.
A lone warrior in a cheerful fight,
With simplicity, you get it right.

No crowded blooms, just you alone,
Creating peace like a soothing tone.
With every sigh, you clear the air,
A soft reminder—come, if you dare!

The world keeps rushing, but you just stay,
In patient stillness, you seize the day.
With a gentle nod, you claim your space,
In graceful solitude, you find your grace.

So here's your toast, you wise old plant,
"Slow down, my friends! Let's just recant."
With laughter sprouting from every vein,
Your quirky spirit, we can't contain!

Surrendering to the Green

In the corner, a foliage queen,
Dressed in white, she's so serene.
I water her like she's a pet,
Hoping for a flower duet.

Her leaves are glossy, she looks so proud,
I whisper secrets—she'll tell the crowd.
Though she never laughs at my jokes,
I swear she's plotting with the oaks.

I trip over pots in the night,
She giggles softly—what a sight!
With roots that dance in silent cheer,
I guess it's clear she's got no fear.

So here I stand, her humble friend,
In a battle I know I won't win.
To a green thumb, this is my quest,
But really, she's the one who's blessed.

Lush Alchemy of Stillness

A plant in the room, oh my what a thrill,
Her blooms like cupcakes, made with skill.
I promise her sunlight, I hope it's enough,
Yet she thrives on my mishaps, how very tough!

I tell her my dreams, she's a great listener,
But talk back? Not a chance, she's a sister.
With roots like fingers, she clings to the earth,
While I spill my coffee, she's quite the mirth.

And when I dance through the living room,
I swear I hear her chuckle, it's like a tune.
A leaf goes fluttering, and the cat meows,
It's a party of silence—who needs a loud?

So cheers to my friend, in her leafy attire,
Both zen and clumsy, we fuel our fire!
I'll keep pouring love, she keeps growing tall,
Together we'll conquer—this house is our hall!

The Cloak of Gentle Peace

In my cozy space, she reigns with grace,
Draped in greens, like a warm embrace.
I swear she rolls her eyes sometimes,
While I sing her tunes and make up rhymes.

Each morning I greet her, "What's the plan?"
She whispers back, "Oh, just be a fan."
With air so fresh, she smiles so wide,
Who knew that plants could be such pride?

A simple worry, how much should I feed?
She rolls her leaves like "I'm good, indeed!"
Twirling my watering can like a wand,
I'm the quirky magician of our little pond.

So here's to the greenery that plays along,
With her gentle spirit, I can't go wrong.
A housemate who listens, all leafy and bright,
In this game of life, she's pure delight.

A Requiem of Serene Blooms

Oh, humble lily, you're quite a star,
In a world of chaos, you shine from afar.
I check on you daily, with utmost care,
Wondering if all plants have this flair.

Your petals like whispers, so soft and sweet,
While I trip on your pot like it's a feat.
You stand there laughing, a stillness so full,
With roots that have grasped every drop, no pull.

And when I chat to you, I feel like a clown,
Pouring my heart out, not wearing a frown.
You nod without speaking, oh leafy wise sage,
In this wild jungle, you're the real page!

So here's a toast to your calming sway,
May I water you gently, each and every day.
For in this green nook, where stillness resumes,
You reign over my heart, blooming like balloons!

Flowing with Botanical Serenity

In the corner it sits, all dressed in white,
Like a ghost at a party, it's pure delight.
It sways with the breeze, and gives me the wink,
Who knew a plant could make me rethink?

A gentle reminder of nature's own grace,
With leaves that could put a smile on your face.
Water it well, but not too much fuss,
It thrives on the chaos, it's a plant full of trust.

It dances and twirls in the bright sunlight,
Making my room feel just oh-so-right.
With each little petal, a giggle takes flight,
A comedic companion both day and night.

So here's to the lily, the peace it brings,
With humor and joy, oh, the happiness sings.
For in its soft whispers, serenity beams,
A plant that can brighten the dullest of dreams.

Legends of the Peaceful Blossom

In a land where the plants secretly plot,
Stands a lily that claims, 'I'm the chillest, not hot!'
With leaves like a cape and blossoms like crowns,
It reigns o'er my room without messing around.

The legend foretold of a flower so bright,
That babbled in laughter, and danced in the light.
For every time I glance at its style,
I can't help but chuckle, oh, stay for a while!

Some say it's a sage, a guru of bliss,
With advice on relaxation, you can't miss.
'Breathe in, breathe out,' it whispers with flair,
As I sit and ponder while twirling my hair.

Now, let it be known, in the tales of the plant,
The peace lily reigns, in its kingdom so grand.
So here's to the laughter, the joy that it brings,
A comical ruler, with floral wings!

The Poetry of Pure Green

In the realm of the flora, a tale unfolds,
Of a wondrous green friend with stories untold.
With soft little petals, so tidy and neat,
Its whimsical ballet gets me right off my feet.

'Water me gently!' it seems to declare,
With a wink and a nod, it's beyond compare.
While bloom after bloom brings joy and some fun,
If happiness blooms, then this plant's number one.

In a world of chaos, somehow it thrives,
Listening to quips, oh how it survives!
With humor embedded in each leafy line,
It giggles and whispers, 'Come, share a glass of wine!'

So raise up your glass to the hibiscus too,
And toast to the laughter that dances so true.
For in a leafy sanctuary, bright and serene,
We find joy in the laughter that dances between.

Tranquility in Every Leaf

Oh, tranquility, you plant of the hour,
With leaves that unfurl, a natural power.
You sway with the music, a bohemian tease,
A funky little dancer, swaying in the breeze.

Each leaf is a whisper, a playful prank,
With roots intertwined, a verdant prankster's rank.
I water your throne, and you thrive with glee,
Oh joyous green blossom, you're so like me!

In moments of stillness, you're never alone,
Chilling like a pro on your leafy throne.
You bring peace to my heart and laughter to life,
Oh, bloom of serenity, a joy without strife.

So here's to the lily, the giggles, the green,
In gardens of humor, let your beauty be seen.
With each softly spoken, tranquility flies,
A laugh in the leaves, oh, happiness lies!

Pure Exhalations of Nature

In a pot, you sit so sprightly,
Leaves like hands waving lightly.
Water me, love me, hold me dear,
With each droplet, I disappear.

You dance with dust, a fine ballet,
Making me laugh at the end of the day.
Your white blooms shout, "It's party time!"
While I pretend to be so sublime.

Roots in water, sipping slow,
You're the green queen, stealing the show.
Neighbors peek, whispering low,
"What's that plant? Where did it grow?"

So here's to you, a leafy delight,
Brightening rooms, day or night.
With a wink and a shimmer, you rule the space,
With your funny little planty grace.

An Interlude with Soft Colors

You're a soft cushion in the room,
Feasting on sunlight, you dispel gloom.
With a sheen that says, "Life's a breeze!"
If plants could talk, you'd say, "Oh please!"

In moments of silence, you giggle and sway,
Pretending to nap throughout the day.
Buzzing bees might envy your style,
As you lounge around in pure plant guile.

Tiny bugs think you're quite the catch,
Landing on leaves, no need to hatch.
You roll your eyes at their audacious flight,
Sipping your water, feeling just right.

Sometimes you frown at my absence,
But when I return, it's pure romance.
Together we bask in the cozy glow,
A plant and a friend, stealing the show.

The Color of Quiet Moments

You chill in the corner, so oh-so-fine,
Draped in whispers, sipping on time.
Your leaves unfurl like a friendly wave,
While I try to keep my sanity brave.

A gentle nudge, did you just yawn?
Your green is a hug every single dawn.
I talk to you, you listen so close,
In our silent chat, we're just morose.

Do you dream of jungles, so far away?
Or sip on sunshine, day after day?
Your soft little petals watch me with glee,
In moments of stillness, you're the plant MVP.

I'd swear you chuckle at my funny ways,
As I dust your leaves, my clumsy ballet.
But here we are, just you and me,
In a world of green, forever carefree.

Meditations in Green

Your leaves hold secrets, I can tell,
They gossip softly, under a spell.
You stretch and sway, a yoga pro,
In a quest for sunshine, go with the flow.

When friends stop by, they whisper in awe,
"What's your secret? You're quite the draw!"
I shrug and smile, just letting it be,
While you play modest, so carefree.

Sometimes I swear you pull a face,
At my eclectic home décor race.
But with every glance, you bless the room,
Wrapping us tight in bright green bloom.

Oh, my leafy buddy, it's pure enjoyment,
In laughter and love, we find an appointment.
With you by my side, life's a fun scene,
In our little kingdom of vivid green.

Lush Cherubs of Peace

In the corner, just so green,
A little plant, quite the scene.
With leaves that sway like gentle elves,
It whispers secrets, to itself.

Dust motes dance in sunny rays,
This leafy hero saves the days.
With humor wrapped in tranquil hues,
It thrives on laughter, not a snooze.

Roots a-tangle, what a mess!
I thought I'd fixed the silliness.
Yet here it grows, a joyful sprout,
Who knew plant life had such clout?

So here's to you, my cheery mate,
With every sigh, I celebrate.
A funny friend, through thick and thin,
You show me joy, let life begin!

Sanctuary of the Silent Flower

Amidst the chaos, there you stand,
A quiet soul, at my command.
With blossoms white, a stony gaze,
You make me chuckle in the haze.

What's your secret? I must know!
Do you practice the art of low?
With roots that wiggle, branches sway,
You're the zen master of my day.

In stillness, you take up space,
With such a calm, an endearing grace.
You listen close, don't laugh or shout,
Just patiently waiting, no doubt!

And when the watering can arrives,
You perk right up, oh how you thrive!
A sanctuary of quiet cheer,
With you around, there's naught to fear!

Gentle Spirals of Growth

In spirals, you twist with glee,
A curious dance, can't you see?
With every leaf, a giggle grows,
Wherever you sway, hilarity flows.

You've tangled my heart, quite the feat,
With roots that wiggle and steal my seat.
In nature's comedy, you're the star,
I chuckle daily, near and far.

Each petal whispers, "What's next, mate?"
Do you hear the snickers, or just sedate?
A playful plant that loves a jest,
In our green kingdom, you're the best!

So let's dance to our funny tune,
Beneath the wink of a bright-lit moon.
Gentle spirals, laughter rings,
In your leafy embrace, joy springs!

Garden of Whispered Dreams

In this garden, where you bloom,
I hear the giggles from every room.
The dreams you weave are pure delight,
With puns and jokes, you're quite the sight!

With every bud, a wisecrack grows,
You wink at shadows, who knows?
In whispered dreams, you laugh with glee,
Does plant life know how to be free?

I'll prune your jokes and cut the puns,
But you just chuckle, oh what fun!
Each snip and tuck, a sly retort,
You're clearly the jester of this court.

Among the herbs and blooms so bright,
You're the king of comedic light.
In this garden, laughter beams,
Thank you, friend, for whispered dreams!

www.ingramcontent.com/pod-product-compliance
Lightning Source LLC
Chambersburg PA
CBHW070317120526
44590CB00017B/2712